Great Truths In Very Plain Language

Ashton Oxenden

In the interest of creating a more extensive selection of rare historical book reprints, we have chosen to reproduce this title even though it may possibly have occasional imperfections such as missing and blurred pages, missing text, poor pictures, markings, dark backgrounds and other reproduction issues beyond our control. Because this work is culturally important, we have made it available as a part of our commitment to protecting, preserving and promoting the world's literature. Thank you for your understanding.

GREAT TRUTHS,

IN VERY PLAIN LANGUAGE.

BY THE

REV. ASHTON OXENDEN,

RECTOR OF PLUCKLEY, KENT.

LONDON:
WERTHEIM, MACINTOSH, AND HUNT,
24, PATERNOSTER-ROW,
AND 23, HOLLES-STREET, CAVENDISH-SQUARE.
1861.

SERMON I.

ABOUT SIN.

Ezekiel xviii. 4.

"The soul that sinneth, it shall die."

I WANT to speak *very* plainly to you in these Sermons. I wish them to be plainer sermons than common. And I shall almost try and forget that you are acquainted with even the leading truths of God's Word. I shall speak just as if I had before me a little group of the most unlearned people I could find.

Mind you then, this will be the main object of these sermons—to be very plain and homely—so plain, that the most ignorant and unlearned *may*, if he pleases, understand every word I say. And if any poor man or woman gets good from these sermons, or if any bad one goes away with a wish to become better, then I shall not feel that I have laboured in vain.

One thing I specially ask you, and that is to lift up your hearts to God, and beg of Him to bless my attempt. O Lord, be with him who speaks, and with those who hear. Give thy blessing for Jesus Christ's sake.

My first sermon will be about *Sin*;

The second, as to *how a Sinner may be saved*;

The third, about *Holiness*;

The fourth, about *Prayer*; and

The fifth, about *Heaven* and *Hell*.

I begin then with a matter which

deeply concerns every one of us—SIN. And I will tell you why it deeply concerns every one of us, because we have all got sin clinging to us, like a hateful disease, which causes us much trouble, and pain, and danger.

Suppose I was to become acquainted with some Family; and I was to find that this family was suffering from some dreadful complaint, which was ruining their health, and spoiling their happiness —not merely one or two of the family, but every member of it, without a single exception. I should naturally ask, How did they all get this fearful disease? Where did it come from? What will be the end of it? Is there any cure for it?

My brother, thou art the man. Thou art one of this unhealthy family. Thou hast this awful disease—a disease within you which has been troubling you ever since you were born. I mean the disease of *sin*. I may call it *a family disease*, for all the family of man have it—none are free from it—as the Apostle says, "All have sinned."

Now, there are three inquiries I want to make—

Where did this disease come from?

What will it lead to?

How can we be delivered from it?

First, Where did this disease come from? This is to be our first inquiry. All diseases come from some cause or another. If a man sits in a draught, he is very liable to catch cold. If he stays in a room with a person who has got a fever, it is more than likely that he will take it. If a Father and Mother have a weakly constitution, how often we see that the children share it with them; they are sickly too. And how is it with *sin?* How did we come by *this disease*, as I have called it?

The first man that God made was Adam, and the first woman Eve. But did God create them at the first with sin in their hearts? No, certainly not. On the contrary, Solomon tells us in the Book of Proverbs that "God made man *upright.*" And we read too, in the first chapter of the Bible, that "God saw everything that he had made, and behold it was *very good.*" It was not sinful, but good. There was no flaw in God's work. It was all perfect. And again we are told, in that same chapter, that man was made "in the *image of God*"—that means pure, and upright, and holy, and sinless.

God made men then entirely without sin. He made them with healthy and perfect bodies, and with holy and sinless souls. This was their happy and blessed state at first. They knew not what sin was. No sinful thought ever troubled their minds, and no sickness or pain disturbed their bodies. Thus for a while they lived a holy and a happy life. God gave them many commands; and it was their delight to obey them all.

This lasted for some time. We are not told how long. It may have been for years. But one day, whilst they were living in the land of Eden, the Devil came to them, in the form of a serpent, and put a grievous temptation in their way. His great object was to ruin their souls, and make them break off from God. Perhaps, if he had begun by at once proposing to them to give up obeying God, they would have been horrified at the idea. They would have said, "No, God is our Father and our Friend; we dare not, and we will not, disobey Him." The Devil knew this well enough; and so he began by degrees, little by little.

It happened that among all the trees

of the place there was *one* which God had strictly charged them not to touch. Indeed He had plainly said, "In the day that thou eatest thereof thou shalt surely die." Upon this very tree then Satan fixes his eyes. He thought within himself, if I can but make them disobey God with regard to this tree, I shall gain my point. So he goes to the Woman, the weaker of the two, and uses all his efforts to make her eat of it. He speaks to her in some such words as these: "Surely you must be mistaken. God could not have given you such a command. This tree, instead of doing you harm, will do you good. It will make you wise; aye, as wise as God himself." This was very tempting; and after a little more persuasion, she was led to look at the fruit as it hung on the tree, and then to touch it, and at last to eat of it, and to give it to her Husband.

Oh, what misery began from that moment! They had disobeyed a plain command of God. You may perhaps say, "It was but a *small* command they broke." No matter; it was an act of disobedience. There was nothing hard in the command; and so much the greater then was their wickedness in breaking it.

And now sin had got into the world. And, from that hour to this, sin has never left it. Adam and Eve became sinners. And every one of us, who has been born since, has come into the world with sin in his heart. And this is what St. Paul means when he says, "By *one man* sin entered into the world."

You see then we have answered the first question, *Where did sin spring from?* It came into the world when Adam was living in Eden. And it has been in the world ever since. Every one of us is tainted with it. No one of us is without it. "There is none righteous (says the Bible); no, not one." We are like a tree which has been struck with blight. And every single branch, without one exception—large and small—high up, and low down—even the little sucker that is just springing up from the old roots—all, I say, are tainted with it. Even David, "the man after God's own heart," said, "Behold I was shapen in iniquity, and in sin did my mother conceive me." And Job asks, "Who can bring a clean thing out of an unclean? Not one." No, the spring, that was so pure 'at first, was made foul; and then, as you might expect, all the streams that flow from it are foul also.

But let me bring this home to you. Do we not see some symptom of this sinfulness of man's nature breaking out, whichever way we turn? Do we not meet with it in all directions?

We will take a Labouring Man, and see how many proofs he has of it, almost every day of his life. He gets up early in the morning; and perhaps the thought comes across him, "Why should I go out to work? Why is labour necessary? Could not the Almighty have made all things to grow without my toiling for it?" Yes, He certainly could. But it is *Sin* that has made labour needful. When Adam sinned, this was one part of his sentence, "In the sweat of thy face shalt thou eat bread."

Well, the Labourer leaves his home, we will suppose. And as he walks on, with his tools on his shoulder, he feels perhaps many an ache. His head pains him, it may be; or his limbs are weary; or he feels unwell in his body. "Why is this?" he asks. "Why should there be any sickness or suffering in the world?" I answer, *Sin* is the cause.

Presently he gets to the field, where his work lies. Perhaps it is a corn-field. And he wonders for a moment, why God should permit the rank grass and weeds to spring up among the wheat and weaken the crops, and cause such endless toil to the tiller of the ground. Or, he goes into a pasture-field. And there, as he sees the cattle feeding, he perhaps observes how the strong animals oppress the weak. "How is all this?" he asks. I answer, *Sin* is at the root of it. This is *a fallen world*, or it would not be so. It was far otherwise in the garden of Eden. There all was peace and harmony and love. There everything grew without hinderance. There were no weeds there. No sickness, no pain, no suffering, were there. What has made the difference? Why *Sin*, has come into the world.

And the consequence is, that "the whole creation (as St. Paul says) groaneth and travaileth in pain together until now." The very ground was cursed for man's sin. Just turn to the third chapter of Genesis, and read God's sentence on Adam, "Cursed is the ground for thy sake; in sorrow shalt thou eat of it all the days of thy life: thorns also and thistles shall it bring forth to thee."

But let us suppose that the Labourer has finished his work, and is returning home. As he passes through his village, it may be, his eyes are saddened, and his ears pained, by a loud curse from the lips of one; or by another reeling out of a public-house; or by a crowd of men quarrelling about some trifling matter. "Ah," he may think within himself, "this could never have been intended by God. Surely it was not so at the first. There was then no drunkenness, no quarrels, no strife." No; but man sinned, and departed from God, and all these evils have been the sad consequence.

At length the Workman enters his own quiet cottage, and sits down to his humble meal. His family are all gathered around him, and perhaps his Wife is sitting there, with a little one in her arms. He looks at it, and sighs as he feels how soon that little one will begin to go wrong; how hard it is to teach it what is right; how readily it will fall into bad ways. Nay, *even now* it shows signs of evil temper, restlessness, and disobedience. God did not make it so, he knows. And yet scarcely a day passes, that he does not have some plain proof that *Sin* is bound up in the heart of his child.

Does not then our every-day life prove to us just what we may learn from our

Bibles—that man is *a sinful, fallen being*, and that the world he lives in is *a sinful, fallen world?*

But now for the *Second* question, WHAT DOES SIN LEAD TO? WHAT IS THE END OF IT?

God threatened Adam, that if he disobeyed Him, DEATH should be his punishment—"In the day that thou eatest thereof (that is, of the forbidden tree) thou shalt surely *die.*" And we know that he did die. And all we who are his children die too. You may have known very old men and women—some living to ninety or a hundred years. But did you ever know any one live on through three or four generations, and never die at all? No; we stay here a few years, and then the sentence falls upon us—DEATH.

But Death of the Body is not all that

sin has brought with it. There is a worse death than that—THE DEATH OF THE SOUL IN HELL! ETERNAL DEATH!

I will tell you then what the end of sin is. It is MISERY *here*, and HELL *hereafter!*

Dear Brethren, let me speak very openly to you. The more affection I feel for you, the more plainly I wish to deal with you. We must not mince matters. It is my duty to speak out. Well then, I solemnly tell you, that if you are at this moment living in sin— yielding to it—giving way to it—indulging in it—if sin has dominion over you —if it has got possession of you—if you go on knowingly committing any one sin —then ETERNAL DEATH IS YOUR PORTION. Every day you live, and every step you take, is bringing you nearer to Hell. It is not merely I who tell you so. St. Paul tells you so, when he says, "The wages of sin is DEATH." And God himself tells you so in the text, "The soul that sinneth, it shall DIE"—die eternally —die for ever.

And is sin so sweet to you, that it is worth while to enjoy it for a few short days at such a fearful price? Stop, sinner—stop in your course. Remember, you can't live for ever; and the sure wages of sin is death. Is it worth while, do you think, to serve Satan for such wages as this? Just make a calculation. Put on one side a life of sin—shall I say, with all its pleasures and enjoyments? I do not believe there are any. But if you please, say—with all its pleasures and enjoyments. And then set down over against it the agonies of the lost, "the worm that never dieth," and "the fire that shall never be quenched." And now tell me, Are not "the pleasures of sin for a season" purchased at a *ruinous* price?

ABOUT SIN.

If then you are living a careless and sinful life, let me tell you again that the end of these things is DEATH. There may be a pleasure in sin for the moment; but does it not leave a sting behind it? It may be sweet to the taste; but is there not wormwood and gall with it? I therefore say to you, in the words of the Hymn,—

 Hasten, Sinner, to be wise;
 Stay not for the morrow's sun;
 Wisdom if you still despise,
 Harder is she to be won.

 Hasten, Sinner, to return;
 Stay not for the morrow's sun;
 Lest thy lamp should cease to burn,
 Ere the needful work is done.

 Hasten mercy to implore:
 Stay not for to-morrow's sun;
 Lest thy season should be o'er,
 Ere to-morrow is begun.

Lord, do Thou the sinner turn;
Rouse him from his senseless state;
Let him not thy counsel spurn,
And lament his choice too late.

But there is a *Third* question which I am to answer; and a most important one it is. Is THERE ANY CURE FOR THIS DISEASE? In other words, Is there any way by which the sinner may be saved? Is there any safety for us—any deliverance from the Hell which we so richly deserve?

Man has sinned. We have all sinned. If then I hate sin, and am anxious about my soul, is there any salvation offered to me? There is no way of escaping bodily sickness and death. We must all pay *that* penalty. But the death of the *soul* we *may* escape.

When Adam had sinned, God did not leave him to perish. Neither did He bid him find his own way to heaven. But, in His great mercy, He showed him how he might escape from the misery he had brought down upon himself. He made known to him that a Saviour would be sent. And, thank God, you have often heard and read about this Saviour. You know that He has come and died for sinners, and that He is now ready to receive, and bless, and pardon all who come to Him. "God so loved the world that he gave his only-begotten Son, that whosoever believeth in him should not perish, but have everlasting life." And now I tell you again, that there is but one way to heaven—but one salvation—but one Rock to rest upon—but one hiding-place to shelter yourself in—and that is Christ. He is the Sinner's Friend, and the Sinner's Hope. "There is none other name under heaven, given among men, whereby we must be saved."

But I hope to say more on this bright

and blessed subject in my next plain sermon.

Now, then, a few words more, and I have done. You have heard in this sermon about *Sin*—how that we have every one of us sinned against God. Well then, here is something to start with. Get this clear upon your minds, and you will have learnt something. When you go home, say to yourself, "I have sinned. Yes, whatever man may think of me, and whatever I may have thought of myself up to this time, the truth must be told—I am a sinner in God's sight."

Now perhaps Satan will come and whisper in your ear, "You have *not sinned much.*" Be it so; still God's word says, "The soul *that sinneth* it shall die." Or, perhaps he will try to quiet your conscience, by making you feel that you are *not worse than others.* It may be so; but will not others perish, if they have not found salvation? Or, again, he may tempt you to feel easy, because *God is merciful,* and He will not therefore be strict in punishing sin.

Do not listen to him. *You* have sinned; and God will reckon for every sin, great and small, open and secret. Just think, how many wrong things you have done—how many right things you have left undone—how many foolish, idle, light words you have spoken—how many bad thoughts have lodged within you— how many evil wishes and desires have sprung up in your heart! Surely even *the best* of us have a tremendous account to render in: how must it be then with *the worst?* And if all your sins are unforgiven, what will become of you?

Take my advice then. Hasten to Christ. Go to Him, and tell Him of your sins, and ask Him to release you from them. You cannot go to Him *with your body,* for He is no longer upon earth —He is in heaven. But what I mean is, go to Him *with your heart,* and speak to Him with your lips. There He is above, though we see Him not. He is ready to listen to your cry. His blood alone can cleanse you. Take your sinful bad heart to Him, and ask Him to change it. Take your heavy debt to Him, and entreat Him to stand surety for you. He is able to give you deliverance—peace and joy here, and everlasting life in heaven.

SERMON II.

SALVATION FOR THE LOST.

MATTHEW XVIII. 11.

"The Son of man is come to save that which was lost."

You will remember that I told you last Sunday that I meant, if God permitted me, to preach to you five very plain sermons. I will try, Brethren, *on my part*, to speak so that the dullest may understand me. But then there is something to be done *on your part;* and that is to give me your whole attention; or else you will get no good. And further, I will ask you, when you leave church, to go over again in your minds what you have heard, so that you may let nothing slip.

Last Sunday, if you recollect, I spoke to you on the words, "The soul that sinneth it shall die." I told you that sin, like a fearful disease, runs through the whole world. I showed you where it springs from—from Adam's disobedience; and also what it leads to—misery here, and eternal punishment hereafter. And then I said just a few words about the way in which we may be delivered from it.

I shall this afternoon say something more about this deliverance. SALVATION FOR THE LOST—this shall be our subject to-day. And may God bless it to us all!

The text sets before us very clearly our state. We are *lost*. It is a *lost* state. It tells us also how we can be saved from this state.

I shall speak to you then on these two points.

First, Our lost state; and,

Secondly, How we may be saved from it.

Now then for the first point we are to consider. We are told in the text what our state is—WE ARE LOST. This is a strong way of speaking, but none too strong, or else we should certainly not have found it in God's Word. But perhaps St. Matthew is here describing the worst of men—just *the very worst*—when he speaks of them as *lost*. No, he is describing man generally—all men—and you and me among the number. As far as we ourselves are concerned, we are lost, ruined, and guilty. God says in the thirteenth of Hosea, "Thou hast *destroyed thyself.*" And we have just been owning as much, and grieving over it in our prayers, "We have erred and strayed from thy ways like *lost* sheep."

We are lost in two ways—doubly lost. We are born into this world with a sinful nature; and so we are lost: "we are by nature the children of wrath." And then, instead of recovering ourselves, we have made ourselves tenfold worse by the sins which we have actually committed.

Suppose you or I had been heaping up stones ever since we were able to use our hands—if it was only one stone a day—would it not by this time be a large heap indeed? Now, not a day has passed, since we knew right from wrong, that we have not sinned. We have been daily adding to the dark black heap of sin; so that we find the Lord saying to us, "Your sins are grown up unto the heavens."

You hardly believe me perhaps. You

think I am taking the worst view of things. You say to yourself, Surely he is making out our state to be a little worse than it really is. No, Brother, I am taking the Scripture view, God's view, the only true view.

It may be, you don't know what sin is. I'll tell you what sin is. Committing murder, Robbery, Getting drunk, Swearing, Telling lies, Breaking God's Sabbaths: these are sins. But I have not told you all. I have not read out one quarter of the list. Every wicked and idle word that has come out of our lips is a sin. Every evil thought is a sin in God's sight; yes, and every bad wish and desire. All are sins in God's eyes. There are many things which the world takes no account of, which the world winks at, but a pure and holy God sees them to be very sinful. There are many secret, hidden, heart-sins, which our fellow-men never noticed. All these, too, are noted down by God, and reckoned against us.

Now I ask you, Brother, is there not many a thing which you did wrong in secret, and which you would never have done if others had seen you? Still God's eye was upon you all the while, and marked that sin.

Then, too, when you have been with those who have either done or said what you knew to be wrong, have you never chimed in, because you were afraid to be different from those about you? Then, let me tell you, you committed a sin—a great sin—against God.

And again, there are many who would shrink back from committing open glaring sins, and yet we find them doing things that are *not strictly honest*. They will overreach a neighbour, just to get a turn in their own favour. Or they will say what is not exactly true, if it will help them out of a difficulty. But this too is a plain sin against God.

Once more, there is such a thing as *intended* sin, which may never be actually committed. Have you never thought of doing, and meant to do, what was wrong; and then something stopped you from doing it? Well then, you were guilty. You had all *the will* to commit sin, though you had not *the opportunity*.

I could go on much further; but I have said enough. I must stop. Perhaps you now see many things to be sinful, which you never counted so before. It is not merely doing outwardly, with the hands, or with the feet, or with the tongue, what is wrong—but it is also thinking, desiring, wishing what is wrong. And even more than this—leaving undone what we should have done.

Oh then, how many, and how great,

are our sins! How fearful is the list! Does not the Apostle speak rightly, when he says, "In many things we offend *all*"—all of us? Surely you must acknowledge that we have all sinned — that there is not one man, woman, or child, among us that has not sinned. Yes, and there is hardly a day in our lives that we have not done something wrong. The heap has been getting higher and higher. The list has been getting longer and longer. Our guilt has been growing deeper and deeper, day by day.

Now, you remember (do you not?) what our Text told us last Sunday. It told us that "THE SOUL THAT SINNETH IT SHALL DIE." Then, do we not *all* deserve to die? Have we not *all of us* forfeited God's favour, and shut ourselves out from heaven? Most true it is that we are fallen, lost, and ruined. Ah, *so fallen*, that we have not strength in ourselves to recover our footing—*so lost*, that we have no power of our own to save ourselves—*so ruined*, that no earthly remedy can restore us. What! save *ourselves!* Can a guilty culprit, condemned to die, save himself? Has he power to tear off the heavy chains that bind him hand and foot? Has he strength to snap asunder the iron bars of his dungeon? Just as powerless is the sinner. If we could live from this moment to the day of our death without committing a single sin, still there is the guilty past to be blotted out, and how can we do that?

Oh then who will deliver us? How can we escape? How can we gain that heaven that we have lost? How can a poor ruined sinner, under sentence of death, be restored to God's favour?

Hear the good news which St. Matthew tells us in our Text. A SAVIOUR has been sent from heaven—a SAVIOUR has come to deliver us—" to save that which was lost." And St. Paul says, "When we were yet without strength, in due time, Christ died *for the ungodly;*" "God commended his love towards us, in that *while we were yet sinners* Christ died for us."

My Brother, if you were sick, and you were told of a remedy that would cure you, would it not be joyful news to you? Here is a remedy for your sick soul. If you were in debt—so hopelessly in debt that you saw no prospect of getting clear—and you were told of some kind Friend, who out of sheer love to you had gone to every one of your Creditors, and had satisfied them all, should you not feel most thankful?

Well, here is all this, and much more —a cure for your soul, a pardon for your guilt, payment for the great debt you owe to God. God "spared not his own Son, but freely delivered him up for us all." Jesus, the sinless One, died for sinners. Our sin was great, but God's mercy was greater.

But you will say, perhaps, "How can I get to the Saviour, and obtain this deliverance? I feel that He only can save me. But how can I lay hold of His mercy, and make it mine? He is up in heaven, and I am on earth. Oh, if I was near Him—if I could know that He had been seen in some neighbouring country—yea, in the most distant country upon earth—I would hasten to Him, and cast myself down at his feet. I would tell Him of all my guilt. I would entreat him to show mercy to a penitent sinner. But I cannot do this; for Jesus is on his throne above. What then must I do to be saved?"

Believe, my Brother, on the Lord Jesus Christ, and thou shalt be saved. Go to this Saviour in prayer. Go to Him this night. Just tell Him what you need, and beg of Him to receive you. He is in heaven; but still He is the Saviour of the lost. He is willing to be *your* Saviour. He is just as able to save you, as if you could see Him before you, with his loving arms stretched out to welcome you. "Him that cometh unto me (He says) I will in no wise cast out." He is seated on His heavenly throne. But is His heart less loving than it once was? Is not His compassion for sinners as great as when He was upon earth? "Is his hand shortened that it cannot save, or his ear heavy that it cannot hear?"

Here is indeed a great salvation. It is great enough to cover every sin that you have ever committed. But have you *laid hold of it?* A boat is a good thing to save a drowning man: but he must *get into it*, must he not? If you are sick, medicine is a fine thing to recover you: but it will be of no use unless you *take it*. And so here is a great and blessed salvation for us: but we must *accept it* with all our hearts.

Have you done so? Are you a saved man? Are you one of those lost ones, whom "the good Shepherd" has found? Or, are you content to live on with all your sins upon you, but with a Saviour far from you? When He looks upon you, does He say, "I have called, but ye refused; I have stretched out my hand, but no man regarded"? Or can He say of you, "I have found my sheep that was lost. This my son *was* dead, and is alive again; he *was* lost, and is found"?

I said just now, that the sinner is lost as far as he himself is concerned—he cannot save himself—he is ruined. But how few of us feel that we are thus lost. How few are uneasy at the thought, and are really anxious about their safety. We don't feel our sins to be great, and therefore we have no desire to be freed from them. Just as a man may be in debt, without knowing it; or may have a deadly disease within him, and all the while fancy himself well. And what is the consequence? Why, he will be quite satisfied to remain as he is—he will feel no anxiety for deliverance.

One great thing we want, Brethren, is to be brought to *know* and *feel* our guilt; for till then, there will be no anxious concern about our souls. Now, it is the Holy Spirit alone who can teach us this. He must touch our hearts by His grace. No one can feel what sin really is—can know the plague of his own heart—and be really concerned about his state—unless God opens his eyes. He may talk of sin; but it will not grieve him. He may see it in his neighbour clearly enough; but he is blind to it himself, unless the Holy Spirit lifts up the curtain, and shows him what he really is, and brings the truth home to his heart.

A man, who has not God's grace in his heart, is like a limb frozen with the cold—it has no feeling in it. What is an idle word to such a man? Why, it is soon spoken and soon forgotten. What is a lie in his sight? It is only what numbers tell every day. What is a broken Sabbath? A thousand excuses are ready for it. What is an act of dishonesty? It is nothing to a man who has not the fear of God before his eyes.

But how very differently we feel, when our souls are awakened, and we see things in their true light! Then every past sin rises up against us with its full force. We see this and that to be sinful, which never troubled us before. We see that God is holy, and that we are unholy. We feel, in short, that the only word that suits us is that word in our Text, "*lost:*" we are *lost!*

This is the state, Brethren, that we must all come to, if we would be saved. It is the state which I hope you will come to. To such the Saviour is welcome. It was to save such that He came—" to save that *which was lost.*"

If you are but brought to feel this, then I am sure you will also feel that Christ is just what you want—He is just the very Saviour for you. Your hard frozen heart will give way. It will melt. The tear of sorrow will trickle down your cheek. Once you thought little of sin. You knew it was a wrong thing; but it never troubled you. You thought little of

Christ. You heard of Him, and read of Him, and perhaps His name sometimes passed through your lips. But that was all. He was nothing to you. But now, if the Holy Spirit has reached your heart, you will no longer think, and feel, and act as you have done.' Sin will be a burden to you. You will feel its heavy weight. You will long to get rid of it. Christ will now be everything to you—your Hope—your Refuge—your All.

My dear Brethren, you may not have much learning. But you have learning enough to know this—that you have sinned, and that you cannot go to heaven *with your sins;* you know you cannot. They must be got rid of, and you must become a holy man, or else the gate of heaven will be for ever closed against you.

There is not an hour for you to lose. Pardon must be got. Your sins must be blotted out. And it is only the blood of Christ that can do this. Seek Him now, when He may be found. Ask Him, entreat Him, beseech Him to save you. Kneel down before Him, and say, "Lord, save me, or I perish: pardon me, or I am lost for ever. Blot out all my sins; and give me grace to become from this moment thy true servant."

And oh, what happiness to be forgiven! to feel that your soul is accepted! and that all is well! Then you will have peace within—a rejoicing, happy heart. Then too you will feel a strong love for Christ; and instead of clinging to this world, and dreading the hour when you must leave it, you will long to dwell with Him who has saved you, in the Home which He has prepared for His people.

SERMON III.

HOLY AND HAPPY.

Leviticus xx. 7.

"Be ye holy."

There is one mark which stamps every one of God's true children. They may be very different in many respects. Some of them may have learning, and others none. Some may be rich people, and others altogether poor. Some may be old and grey-headed persons, and others just beginning life. But *all* God's real children are holy. They have all this blessed family mark about them—*they are holy people.*

If a man talks ever so well, and yet does not act well; if he attends church regularly, and reads his Bible, and even comes to the Lord's Table; and yet lives about as others live—no better, and no holier—in short, if he has not this mark, then you may be quite sure that man is *not* a true child of God.

How was it with the good men we read of in the Bible? Were not Abel, and Enoch, and Abraham, and St. Paul, and John the Baptist, holy men? Certainly they were. They all had *the mark*. They hated sin; and what they seemed always to be aiming at was to be walking in the path of holiness.

Now, it may be well that I should tell you what is meant by being holy; and then I will show you how we sinners may become holy.

WHAT IS IT TO BE HOLY THEN?

1. A holy man *fears God*. He feels all the day long that there is a great God above him, who watches all his actions, knows all his thoughts, and hears every word he speaks. He feels that he himself is but a poor weak creature, and that God can either give him health, or lay him down on a bed of sickness when He pleases; that He can either give life, or take it away from the strongest of us in an instant. And above all, with regard to his *soul*, he feels that God can either save it, or destroy it for ever.

Now, all this makes him *fear* God. The wicked are bold enough to despise God. They are even so daring, many of them, as to say in their hearts, "What is the Almighty, that we should serve him?" Ah, they do not consider that He could in one moment crush them to powder. He could in an instant stop them short in their wicked course, and summon them into His presence. But their eyes are blinded; and so they go on from bad to worse, putting death, and judgment, and eternity, far from them.

But a good man is far wiser, and far happier. He lives "in the fear of the Lord all the day long." He knows that God is everywhere. He has a constant feeling that God is near him. He seems to see Him in everything. He loves Prayer, because then he can speak to God. And he loves his Bible, because there God speaks, as it were, to him.

Surely this is just what you and I ought to feel, Brethren. And Solomon tells us in the Book of Proverbs, that this is the way to be happy, "Happy is the man (he says) that feareth alway."

2. Then, again, a holy man *loves God*.

He not only fears Him, but loves Him also. You know what it is to love a Friend. Your heart is turned towards him. You like to be often thinking of him, and to have him often with you. It is a pleasure to you to do what he wishes. If he is despised, it grieves you. If he is spoken against, you stand up for him.

So it is, if we love God. Our hearts will be given to Him. Whilst many hearts are drawn to the world, ours will be for ever turning to that dearest Friend in heaven. You know what a Compass is. It is an instrument which Sailors use at sea, to know in which direction to steer their ships. If you have ever seen a compass, you have noticed a little spindle or needle, which always points towards the north. Whichever way you place the compass, the needle is sure to spin round, and turn towards the north.

Just so the heart of a holy man is always turning in the same direction— namely, towards God. He feels a power within which is continually drawing his heart upwards. He is often thinking of God. Like the miser, his thoughts are for ever dwelling on his treasure. And as *his* treasure is in heaven, "there will his heart be also."

3. Then, too, a holy man *feels a pleasure in doing God's will.* If you have got an earthly Master whom you love, do you not take a real delight in doing what he wishes? Is it not a pleasure to you to work for him? I am sure many of you know what this feeling is. And so, if you love God with all your heart, you will not feel that it is a trouble and a task to you, but a pleasure, to do His will. It is true, we have all by nature a will of our own; but a good man will be always trying to

overcome that, and to do the will of his heavenly Father. God's commands are his rule; and his great desire is to follow that rule in all he does. He tries to find out what God's will is, and then he endeavours to do it, whether it is pleasant to him or difficult.

In short, a holy man desires to walk in that path which the Gospel marks out for him, turning neither to the righ nor to the left. He shrinks from everything sinful, and hates what God hates. If he sees a thing to be wrong, that is quite enough for him: he will have nothing to do with it. And thus, in little things, as well as in great things, he is careful not to offend his gracious God.

Ah, Brethren, it is a narrow path that the Christian must walk in, if he wishes to live a holy life, and if he wishes to be hereafter in that place which Christ has prepared for His beloved people.

Are *you* in that path? Are you fighting against sin, and striving to reach heaven? Depend upon it, without this striving you will never get there. Oh, how many there are who are living an easy life — not perhaps an openly wicked life—but still an easy careless life. They eat, and drink, and sleep. They go on much the same one day as another. They do pretty much as others do. And they think they shall fare as others fare. They walk, as the Bible says, " according to the course of this world." Alas! there is no heaven for such. They will never win the prize; for without holiness, we are told, " no man shall see the Lord."

But let us now inquire, " How WE MAY BECOME HOLY. To lead a holy life is indeed to live a happy and blessed life. How then can we be made holy? How can a sinful man be changed into a holy man?

In my other two Plain Sermons I tried hard to impress upon you that we are all by nature sinful. Your ears must indeed have been dull of hearing, if you did not take in at all events that sad truth — that we all have a sinful and corrupt nature. Well then, this sinful nature must be changed. Our hearts, and affections, and desires, must all be changed, or else we can never be right with God.

But can we change our own hearts, do you think? Try to do it, and you will fail. Can Ministers change their people's hearts? Oh no; else an earnest good Minister would be quite sure to have a holy flock around him; for nothing he desires so much as to see

F

them all holy. No, this is God's work, and not man's; it is the work of the Holy Spirit.

Do not think that it is enough to be a little altered in the outer man. If a tree is withered, it is not enough to lop off a few dead branches from it. It must be dug about, and dunged. The soil must be changed. The disease must be overcome. The tree must become healthy; or else it will never bear any good fruit. And sinful man too must be changed—altogether changed, within and without. He must be converted by God's grace. A vast and thorough change must be wrought in him by the almighty power of God. This is what Jesus meant, when He said to Nicodemus, "Except a man be *born again*, he cannot enter into the kingdom of heaven."

What a work is this! It was a great

work for God to *make* us at the first. But it is, I think, a still greater work to *new*-make us. And yet nothing short of this will do. Without it we cannot serve the Lord here, nor be with Him hereafter.

Do you not, Brethren, sometimes feel inclined to go wrong, when you wish to go right? Have you never seen a thing to be sinful, and yet you have a strong desire to go and do it? Have you never had a great wish to get to heaven, and yet no wish to walk in the narrow road that leads to it? How is this? Why, it is the badness of your heart that keeps you back. And does not this show you, that that bad heart of yours must be got rid of, and a new heart given to you?

And can *my* heart be thus changed? perhaps you will ask. Yes, it can. And I will tell you *by what means* this mighty change is usually brought about.

1. In some God works a change *by the preaching of his Word.* St. Paul says, "Faith cometh *by hearing,* and hearing by the Word of God." And St. Peter speaks of our being born again, not of corruptible seed, but of incorruptible, *by the Word of God.*" A man, we will say, comes to church thoughtless and unconcerned; and perhaps he hears something that goes home to his very heart—something that arouses him, and makes him think. And he goes away determined to break off his sins, and to lead a very different life. This may be the case with some of you to-day. God grant that it may be so! And whose doing would it be? If any man or woman became changed owing to this sermon, *whom* would he have to thank? Not me, but God, who, if He sees fit, can make

use of my poor words to touch your heart.

Oh then, come to God's house. Come, you who are thoughtless, careless, worldly-minded. Come, you who have little or no learning—we will try and teach you something for your good. Come all—it may be, you will carry away something, which may be the saving of your soul.

2. *Reading the Bible* too, and other religious books, is very often the means of awakening men, and leading them into a new and better path. If you will only take God's Book, and ask the Lord Himself to teach you, I am very sure that you will find a blessing.

3. *The Season of Sickness* again, is often a most blessed time for a man's soul. He then begins to think. Death and eternity come before him. He feels that he is a dying creature. He is alarmed perhaps about his soul, and earnestly

cries out, "What must I do to be saved?" So you see, dear Brethren, that sickness and trouble oftentimes are a great blessing. They are painful to bear, and we would be glad to be without them. But many times they prove to be our greatest mercies. So King David felt, when he said, "It is good for me to have been afflicted. Before I was afflicted I went wrong, but now have I kept thy word."

4. But there is another means, which never fails. "What," you will say, "does he who uses it *always* get what he wants? Can you tell me of any method by which I can *make sure* of getting this blessed change?" Yes, I can tell you of a method, which I believe, never fails—a method which is within the reach of all, and which every one may use. I mean *Prayer*—earnest prayer from the heart.

I am certain that no one ever yet

prayed earnestly that the Holy Spirit would change his heart, without his prayer being granted. God promises to do it; for He says, "*A new heart* will I give you, and *a new spirit* will I put within you; and I will take away the stony heart out of your flesh, and give you *a heart of flesh*"—which means a softened heart. And again, we have this plain promise from Christ, "Your heavenly Father will give the Holy Spirit to them that ask him."

Now, let us just gather up what has been said in this sermon. You have heard *what it is to be holy*—it is to fear God, to love Him, to obey Him, and to be like Him. I have shown you too, that, in order to become holy, *you must be changed*. And I have spoken also of the different ways in which *this change is commonly brought about*—sometimes by the hearing or reading of God's Word; at other times by a fit of illness; or again, in answer to our prayers.

Do you wish then to be a holy and a happy man? You may become so. Only ask for this change, and it will surely be given you. Entreat God for a new heart. Pray that the Holy Spirit may dwell within you, and make you holy. Say, as David did, "Create in me a clean heart, O God, and renew a right spirit within me."

Oh, if I could only bring you on your knees—if I could only lead you to pray—all would soon follow. God's work would go on within you, and you would soon become a very different person—much better, much holier, much happier.

But let us take one more look at the

Text. God says, "Be ye holy." It is *a command*, you see. It is God's will that every one of us should be holy. And why so? Not because He is anything the happier for our being holy. If all the world were as bad as sin could make them, *He* would still be happy in heaven. But He calls on us to be holy, because He knows that if we are holy, *we* shall be happy also.

Did you ever know a wicked man to be a happy man? He may laugh, and sing, and talk, and be merry now and then—I do not deny that. But is he really happy within himself? No; I think not. And how is it with *you?* Which have been your happiest moments —when you knew you were sinning against God, and your conscience told you that He was angry with you? or, when you were doing what was right? I am sure that those have been your best and brightest moments, when you have walked in the ways of God. If I could know all, and had your hearts open before me, I should find that sometimes sin makes you very miserable. Truly does the Bible speak, when it says, "The wicked are like the troubled sea when it cannot rest. There is no peace, saith my God, to the wicked."

Look at the man who is living for this world—seeking pleasure here, and gain there—living without God, and without Christ—breaking the Sabbath—neglecting the Bible—seldom or never praying. Is there happiness in that man's heart? Is there any peace there? We know there can be none.

But take another man—one whose heart is really given to God—a really religious man. He is always seen in God's house. He loves his Sundays better than all the other days in the week.

He prizes his Bible. He delights in Prayer. He walks in God's ways. In short, he is a holy man. And can you doubt whether such a man is happy or no? Would you not be glad to be as happy as he is? Though you may perhaps be foolish enough to laugh at him for being religious, yet I know you would change places with him, if you could.

Then do you not see that the holy man is a happy man? And this is why God says to all of us, "Be ye holy."

But there is another reason. Without being *holy now*, we cannot be *with God hereafter*. God is a holy Being, and heaven is a holy place. Nothing unclean can enter there. Only "the pure in heart shall see God." Do you not yourselves feel, that with an unchanged heart you would be utterly out of place in God's presence? If you have no taste for His service on earth, how completely unfit you must be for His service in heaven.

Now, my dear Friends, if you wish to be happy, pray to God to make you holy. Say to Him, " O Lord, I have followed sin too long: give me grace to leave it off, and to become thy true servant. May I from this hour lead a new life." Then I am very sure, you will become a happy man. And then too you may hope to dwell for ever with that Saviour, in whose presence, we are told, " there is fulness of joy, and at his right hand pleasures for evermore."

SERMON IV.

PRAYER.

Psalm lv. 17.

"Evening, and morning, and at noon, will I pray, and cry aloud; and he shall hear my voice."

I AM going to speak to you in this sermon about Prayer. It is a solemn subject. May He who loves prayer, and answers prayer, be with us, and teach us all how to pray.

As I have a great many things to say, I shall divide my sermon in this way—

1st. What is prayer?
2dly. Why should we pray?
3dly. How should we pray?

4thly. Where should we pray?
5thly. When should we pray?
6thly. What should we pray for?

First of all, WHAT IS PRAYER? Let us clearly understand what we mean when we talk about praying.

If any one of your Neighbours is able to give you something that you particularly want, what do you do? Why, you go and ask him for it; and the more you want it the more earnestly do you ask for it. If, for instance, there is a piece of garden ground that you wish for, or a house that you think would just suit you, you go and ask the owner to let you have it. Or, again, if you have got into trouble with your Master by doing something wrong, do you not go and beg him to forgive you? And the more the matter weighs on your mind, the more eager and urgent you are in your request.

Now, just put *God* in the place of

man, and there you have prayer. Prayer is asking God for something, begging, beseeching, entreating, Him to give you something.

But you may think perhaps that it is altogether a different thing asking a man, *whom you can see*, for anything, and praying to God, *whom you cannot see*. Do we then never ask a person for anything without seeing him? Do we never send a message, or sit down and write to a person, though he may be a long way off—even in a different country? And yet we feel pretty sure that our petition will reach him. We are told that the post will carry our letter, and that in a short time it will get to him. We believe this, and so we send off our letter.

And when you pray to an unseen God, you must believe. God tells you that he can, and will, hear your prayers.

And ought you for a moment to doubt Him? I will just read out to you a few of these promises, as they are given to us in the Bible.

In the 145th Psalm, David says, "The Lord is nigh unto all them that call upon him. *He also will hear their cry.*"

In the 29th of Jeremiah the Lord says, "Then shall ye call upon me, and ye shall go and pray unto me, and *I will hearken unto you.* And ye shall seek me, and find me, when ye shall search for me with all your heart."

And in the New Testament Jesus says, "Ask, and *it shall be given you.*" "All things whatsoever ye shall ask in prayer, believing, *ye shall receive.*" And, again, "Whatsoever ye shall ask the Father in my name, *he will give it you.*" And these are the words of St. John, "This is the confidence that we have in him, that if we ask anything according to his will, *he heareth us.*"

Here then you have God's own word for it, that your prayers will be answered. Therefore, whenever you kneel down to pray to Him, be just as sure that He hears you as if you could see Him. For He is not like one of us; but He is a Spirit. His eyes are in every place, and his ears can hear every whisper. Nay, there is not a thought in our hearts, but He knoweth it altogether.

Then, how different too is God from our fellow-men in another respect. They sometimes *refuse altogether* to give us a hearing. Sometimes it is *not in their power* to grant our petitions. And sometimes they *might* give us what we ask for, but they are *not willing.* But God is always *ready* to listen to us. He is *able* to give us all that we ask for, and more besides. Yes, and He is *willing* too, if we ask for what is good for us, and if we ask in a proper manner.

This is very encouraging. We may go to God like children to a Father, and be quite certain that He has an attentive ear to listen to all our wants. Try and feel this the next time you pray. Say to yourself, "The God I am going to pray to is not a Stranger, that I need shrink from Him. He is my Father—my gracious and loving Father—and He will receive me as His Child, and not send me away unheard." "If ye being evil" (said our Lord) "know how to give good gifts unto your children, how much more should your Father which is in heaven give good things to them that ask him."

2dly. WHY SHOULD WE PRAY? Does not God know everything, and cannot He give without my asking? Undoubtedly He can. Indeed the word of

God tells us so; for Jesus says, "Your heavenly Father knoweth what things ye have need of *before ye ask him.*"

What use then is there in praying to Him? There is great use. He requires it of us. He will have us pray, else we should soon forget that all our gifts come from Him. He does not say simply, "I will give you." But He says, "*Ask,* and ye shall have"—"*He that asketh* receiveth,"—"I will yet for this be *inquired of* by the house of Israel to do it for them."

I have now then explained to you *What prayer is*, and *Why we should pray.* It is not because God *needs to be told* of our wants; but because He will have us humble ourselves before Him, and ask Him one by one for all that we require.

Now we come to the third point—How WE SHOULD PRAY. We should pray with *faith*, with *earnestness*, with *understanding*, with *humility*, and *in the name of Christ*. Here are five things necessary, in order to pray rightly.

1. We should pray *with Faith*. Jesus tells us, in those words which I read to you just now, "Whatsoever ye shall ask in prayer, *believing*, ye shall receive." And St. James, when he tells us how a man should pray, says, "Let him ask *in faith*, nothing wavering." Why, it would be a poor way of asking a favour of a fellow-creature to go to him and say, "I hope you will give me so and so, but I very much doubt it." He would look upon it as an insult. And so, when we go to God with unbelieving hearts, though we do not tell Him that we doubt Him, He looks within and knows all. And must it not be displeasing to Him to have His power questioned, or His willingness to listen to our requests?

Try then, when you pray, to feel that you are in God's very presence. Speak to Him, as if He was standing before you. Take your troubles and your wants to Him, as you would to a dear Friend who has a heart to feel for you, and power to relieve you.

2. Next, you should pray *with Earnestness*. If you saw a common beggar in the street, and he seemed not to care whether you listened to him or not, would you not turn a deaf ear to his petition? Would you not say to yourself, "That man cannot be much in want, or he would be more pressing"? I am afraid that many of our prayers to God are of this sort. Have you not Sunday after Sunday come here, and when we have knelt down to confess our sins and to cry for mercy, you have sat unconcerned? Is this praying? Or, night and morning, at home, you have

repeated a string of words, almost without knowing what you were saying. Is this praying? It is making a pretence of praying—going through the form of it—but there is no prayer in this. Oh, if you felt your wants, and had a strong desire to get them supplied, the case would be very different with you. It was very different with the Publican in the parable. He felt his sins, and longed for pardon; and so there was a living earnestness in that short prayer of his, "God be merciful to me a sinner." It was very different too with Peter, when he was on the water, and in danger of drowning—"Beginning to sink, he cried, Lord, save me." Very different was it too with that poor Leper who, when he saw Jesus, "fell on his face, and besought him, saying, Lord, if thou wilt, thou canst make me clean." And very different with that brokenhearted thief upon the cross, who cast a longing look on the Saviour, and cried out, "Lord, remember me, when thou comest into thy kingdom." Here were men in earnest—here were *heart*-prayers, and not *lip*-prayers only. And these prayers were heard.

My Friends, what we want is more *life* in our souls—more of *God's Spirit* within us. And then there will be more earnestness in our prayers.

"Give us, O Lord, to feel our wants. Quicken these drowsy sleeping souls of ours. And may we never again be guilty of the sin of drawing nigh unto thee with our *lips,* when our *hearts* are far from thee."

3. We should pray also *with Understanding*. What is the use of going to the Lord with words which we do not understand the meaning of? They may

be very fine words, and very good words; but if they are beyond us, it is a mere mockery to offer them up to God.

Some persons are in the habit of using *their own words* in prayer. And if they can do so without difficulty, perhaps it is well. It is true, your words may not be very choice, or very learned; but still, if they flow out of your heart, God will hear them.

But many people cannot do this; and therefore they use the prayers of others. It matters little which plan you adopt. Only pray with your whole heart, and think over the meaning of what you are saying to God.

I once spoke to you in a sermon about using those unmeaning, foolish words which begin with, "Matthew, Mark, Luke, and John, bless the bed that I lay on"—words which I found so many of you using, when I first came into this parish. But I hope that you have long since given them up for some *real* prayer; for this is nothing more than a prayer to the Apostles, and not to God.

I have also spoken to you about using the Belief *as a Prayer*. Now the Belief was drawn up by holy men, and it is a very valuable writing because it tells us what we should believe as Christians; and so we repeat it every Sunday in church. But you will notice that we never say it *upon our knees*, and for this very reason—because it is not a Prayer, and was never intended to be one. Now, remember this. And though there can be nothing wrong in your saying over the Belief in private, if you wish to do so, yet bear in mind that you are not offering up any *prayer* to God.

Most of us, I hope, use the Lord's Prayer every day. And I dare say we have gone on using it ever since we were children. And it is quite right that we should, for it is the very prayer that Jesus gave us. But I am afraid that many do so, without ever thinking, or trying to think, what each petition in that prayer means.

Have we not great reason, Brethren, most of us, to ask God to pardon all our past ignorant unmeaning prayers? And will it not be well for us to make the same resolution for the future as St. Paul made, "I will pray with the spirit, and I will pray with the *understanding* also"?

But in showing you How we should pray, there are two more things I must mention.

4. One is, we should pray with *Humility*. What are we? Mere dust and ashes—mere worms—and worse than this, we are sinful creatures—very sinful in God's sight.

When we draw near to God then we should humble our *hearts*, and we should humble our *bodies* too. Do we act thus? I am afraid not. I am afraid there are several, who when they come to this House of Prayer *never kneel*. Some of the congregation do; but others do not from one year's end to the other. Can this be right? Brethren, if you wish your church-going to be profitable, come here *to pray*. Kneel down before God, and join heartily *in* the prayers that are offered. Some foolish ones may perhaps laugh at you for doing so; but it matters little, if you can only feel that you are doing what is right.

And then, how is it when you pray *at home?* Perhaps there is here and there one of you who do not kneel *even then.* And some too have the bad habit of saying their prayers in bed. Can we call this prayer? Is this the way to put

God off? Have we no more reverence for the King of kings and Lord of lords than this? If you only think a moment, I am sure your own conscience must tell you, that this cannot be the way for a guilty creature to draw near to his heavenly Father.

And if you yourself see it to be wrong, which I hope you do, begin to-night—kneel down on your knees, and humble your heart before the Lord. Let Prayer in future be a real thing with you, and not a mere mock service—an unmeaning form.

5. The *last* direction I shall give, as to how we should pray, is to pray *in the name of Christ*. Why so? Because we are all sinners, and are therefore unworthy to ask anything in our own name. And Christ has come to be our Mediator, to go between us and God.

And He has himself told us that "whatsoever we shall ask the Father *in His name* we shall receive."

Here again is great encouragement. When we feel what unworthy creatures we are, it is no small comfort to know that Christ speaks for us. He will plead for us with His heavenly Father; and *for His sake* we shall be heard.

I have shown you then *how* we should pray—with *faith*, with *earnestness*, with *understanding*, with *humility* (that is, with lowly hearts, and in a lowly posture—on our knees), and also we must ask all *in the name of Christ*.

I can almost fancy some one saying, "Well, if this is prayer, I am sure that mine have been oftentimes no prayers at all. I have merely repeated words, but without feeling my wants, and without really asking my God to supply them. God grant that my prayers in future may be very different from what they have been!"

But now for the other questions, that I am to say a word or two about.

4thly. WHERE should we pray? *This* is the great place for Prayer. God says, "My house shall be called a House of Prayer." Here we should come whenever the doors are opened—not sometimes, but always—not on Sundays only, but on Week Days—not once a day, but twice. What should we think of a Labouring Man who was only willing to work in the afternoons? We should suppose that he had a little private store of his own, and had no need of full wages—that his wants were not very great, and therefore he could do with half-earnings. Ah, my Friends, I must think that you, who come to Church once a day, can have but little knowledge of your own wants. If you felt them more, you would surely come oftener.

But is the House of God the only place in which prayer is heard? What says the Apostle? "I will that men pray *everywhere.*" Pray to Him in your cottage, with your family. Pray to Him in your chamber in private. Pray to Him in the fields, or as you walk along the road.

> "*Where'er* you seek Him, He is found,
> And *every place* is hallowed ground."

5thly. WHEN should we pray? The great times for daily prayer seem to be marked out by David in our Text. He says, "Evening, and morning, and at noon, will I pray, and He shall hear my voice." And Daniel seems to have observed the same custom, for we read of him that he prayed "*three times a day.*"

You *may* have a difficulty in finding a time for prayer in the middle of the day. But never neglect to offer up your prayers morning and night. Get by yourself if you can, and then kneel down, and tell God of your wants, and earnestly ask Him to give you what you need.

Our last question is, "What should we pray for?" We should pray both for earthly and heavenly blessings. God is the Giver of both. You want health for instance, do you not? Then ask the Lord to give it to you. You want work, and kind friends when trouble comes. You need bread for your families. He who feeds the ravens must supply you. He who clothes the lilies must give you raiment. Remember this. We often think, because we can buy food in the village, and get this and that necessary at the shop, and have money to pay for them, we are therefore indebted to no one. Yes, Brother, we are. You and I are just as much indebted to God, as the Israelites were, when He sent them manna from heaven in the wilderness.

But are these things *all* that we want? Are our *Bodies* the only things to think of, and to care about? Have we no *spiritual* wants? no *soul* wants? Have we no pardon to seek? no Saviour to find? no evil heart to keep in check? Do we want no grace? no strength? no Holy Spirit? I never knew a man that was acquainted with his own heart, who did not feel that he greatly needed these spiritual blessings.

Why is it that you have them not? Not because God is unwilling to bestow them—not because you need learning to get them—or because they are only given to just a chosen few—but simply *because you ask not.* Pray more, and I promise that you will have more. There was never yet a real man of God who was not a man of prayer.

Then, dear Brother, if you wish to know God, to love Christ, to be a Christian indeed, and to get to heaven at last, be much in prayer.

How thankful I should be if these plain words of mine led any one of you to make *this* resolution—" From to-day, I will begin by God's help to pray in earnest. I will go, as it were, and speak to my God, and tell Him all my wants. I will kneel down before Him, as one who feels his nothingness. I will not merely have the name of Christ upon my lips; but I will feel that it is for Christ's sake alone that I can be heard."

Now, try to act upon this resolution. It will indeed bring down a blessing. Get into the habit of carrying all your little troubles to your heavenly Father, as well as your great ones—and all your little necessities, as well as your larger ones. I am sure you will find that *this world even* will go better with you. There will be fewer trials weighing you down, and brighter joys to cheer you. You will look up and feel that the Lord is indeed your Friend—that He is concerned for you—that He watches over you, and cares for you. And if you love to speak often to Him on earth, what a happy day that will be, when you shall be with Him, where He is!

I hope to preach to you next Sunday on a still more solemn subject—Heaven and Hell. And that will close my present course of Plain Sermons. May God bless each one of them to your souls, for Jesus Christ's sake!

SERMON V.

HEAVEN AND HELL.

MATTHEW XXV. 46.

"And these shall go away into everlasting punishment, but the righteous into life eternal."

How awful and solemn is our subject to-day—Heaven and Hell! Will you not pray for me, that God will direct my words, so that I may speak as I ought to speak?

Yes, there is a happy Heaven for the saved, and a dreadful Hell for the lost. There is nothing in the Bible more plain than this. There are many difficult things in Scripture which we cannot make out; but this is written as it were with a sunbeam—plainly and clearly.

From our very childhood we have been told that good people go to heaven, and bad people to hell; so that the words HEAVEN and HELL are quite familiar to us all. But have we ever seriously thought what heaven and hell are, and where they are, and how we may escape the one and gain the other? Let us do so now.

1st. *Where is Heaven?* And *where is Hell?* We know not. We are not told in Scripture.

Some people think that Heaven will be *this world made new.* They think so from what St. Peter says in one of his Epistles. He there tells us that at the end of the world, "the heavens shall pass away with a great noise, and the elements shall melt with fervent heat, the earth also and the works that are therein shall be burned up." And then he goes on to say, "Nevertheless we, according to his promise, look for new heavens and a new earth, wherein dwelleth righteousness." Some, I say, gather from these words that our heaven will be *here*. When this world, and all we now see in it, is burned up, they think that God will make a new and more blessed world of it, fit for the joyful abode of His people for ever. It may be so; but God has seen fit to tell us so little on the subject, that a great deal must be only guess-work.

Others, again, think that the stars are all worlds; and that the Christian's home will be in one of those distant stars.

But for the present we must be content to be ignorant as to *where* Heaven is. Now we only "know in part." But if we are God's children, we shall soon know all.

So too with regard to Hell. We know not *where* it is. It is sometimes called "the lower parts of the earth"—"outer darkness"—"the pit of destruction"—"the bottomless pit."

No doubt if it was good for us to know more, God would have told us more. But this we *do* know—that there is a place of unspeakable happiness made ready for God's servants, and there is a place of untold misery prepared for the wicked. And it is of very little use guessing *where* these places are; for with all our searching we shall not find out.

II. But now we turn to a more important point—*What are Heaven and Hell?*

1. Heaven is *God's special abode*. He

is everywhere; but He says, "Heaven is my throne," and we are taught to pray to Him as "our Father who art in heaven." And this is the home too, and the resting-place, of all God's children. It matters very little for us to know *where* Heaven is, so long as we know that God is there, and Christ is there, and that if we are the Lord's people, we shall be there. You remember those comforting words which Jesus Christ spoke, when He saw his disciples sad at the thoughts of His leaving them. He said, "Let not your hearts be troubled. I go to prepare a place for you; and if I go and prepare a place for you, I will come again, and receive you unto myself; that *where I am, there ye may be also.*"

And a little while after, when He offered up that beautiful prayer for his people, He said, "Father, I will that they also whom thou hast given me, be *with me where I am.*"

To be with God himself! To be with Christ! Oh what a glorious thought this is! What an honour! What enjoyment! Ah, my poorer Brethren, you would perhaps feel a little awkward, if you were called to sit down in the company of some rich nobleman, or if you were to be a guest in the Queen's palace at Windsor. And so an ungodly man would feel anything but happy to be with God. But if you are indeed His child—if you love Him, and delight to do His will—then you will feel no strangeness in His presence, you will feel welcome, you will be happy in His blessed company.

To be *with God* then will be one of the chief glories of Heaven.

2. Another is, that there will be *no sin* there. Heaven will be a *sinless* place.

Why is it that we do not love God more? Why do we not love His house more, and His word more, and His day, and His people? Why do we not feel more delight in thinking of Him, and conversing with Him? I will tell you why: because the moment our hearts mount up a little, sin drags us back; it is like a dead weight, that is for ever keeping us down. Why are not God's people more joyful, and happy, and cheerful, even now? Because there is sin dwelling within them. But, thank God, in heaven, sin will no more trouble us. We shall be freed from it for ever. Our love to God and to His people will then be perfect. It will be like light without any darkness, like gold without any dross in it.

3. There will be *no sorrow* in Heaven. It will not only be a sinless state, but it will be also *a sorrowless state*. This

world is a world of trials. It is not merely one thing that troubles us, but a thousand things. Our troubles may come from any quarter. There are the troubles of our Country—troubles in our Family—pains and disease of Body—and sufferings of Mind. Some are happier than others here; but none are perfectly happy. But in the world above there will be "fulness of joy" and "pleasures for evermore." Every tear shall then be wiped away, " and there shall be no more death, neither sorrow, nor crying, neither shall there be any more pain."

4. There will be *delightful employments* in Heaven. Yes, we shall be busy there. There will be no idleness there. If there was, it would not be a happy place for us. We know this from what we feel even here, for it is anything but happiness to be idle. I have often seen a

Labouring Man stopped short in his work, and laid by for a time. Why, the very feeling of idleness is irksome to him. He longs to be at work again. And so it would be a real punishment to the true Christian to say to him, " You must no longer pray, and no longer praise; you must not think any more; nor serve God any more; you are henceforth to be idle for ever."

Thank God, Heaven is very different from this. God has work for His people to do, and work of the most delightful kind. If you look into the Book of Revelation, you will see how St. John describes those happy ones who are in heaven. He says, " They *serve God* day and night in His temple." " They *rest not* day and night, saying, Holy, holy, holy, Lord God Almighty."

Bear this in mind then—if you ever get to heaven, you will be busily employed in doing God's work. And I just ask you, How you can be fitted for His work there, unless you love to work for Him here?

5. But let us pass on now to another very important point—Heaven will be *an everlasting abode.* Those who are once admitted there will no more go out. It is spoken of as " *a continuing* city." Our life there is called " *eternal* life." Our enjoyments there are spoken of as " pleasures *for evermore."* We shall be "*for ever* with the Lord."

Sometimes here on earth we grow fond of certain spots — we love our earthly homes. But there is something continually telling us, that we shall only have them *for a little while.* And are there not beloved ones here, who are dear to us as our own selves—who have twined themselves round our very hearts, as the ivy clings to the tree? Ah, these ties, we know, will all soon be broken. This is a world of separation. But in heaven there will be no partings, no farewells.

Oh, what a difference there is between this world and the next! Everything here is for a time only: everything there is for eternity! Our heavenly joys, our safety, our glory, will be for ever—they will be endless and everlasting.

Brethren, it would be far pleasanter both for me and for you to stop here, and only dwell on this bright and joyous part of the subject. But the picture must be turned round; and we must look at the other side of it. And a very dark side it is. But we must speak of it, sad as it is. For we must remember, there is another abode. And it is well for us to know something about that place also.

Now then, having seen what Heaven is, we come to the inquiry—*What is Hell?*

1. It is *the dwelling-place of the Devil and his Angels.* We are told in the Bible, that it is the place " prepared for the Devil and his angels."

Oh what a thought—to dwell for ever with evil spirits and evil men! Should you like to spend a single night in a madhouse? How would it be, if you were obliged to pass a week in the company of a band of Infidels, from whose lips proceeded only cursing and blasphemy? or to be shut up in a dungeon with a number of men who had committed murder? or to be upon a death-bed, with no other comforters than wicked spirits and reprobate men? And yet this will give you but a poor notion of Hell. I cannot fully describe it to you. I cannot tell you one-half of what it will be to spend the endless years of eternity in so awful a place, and with such awful companions. One's soul shudders at the idea. Is there a single one among us who would not from his heart exclaim, "Lord, save me from such a portion?"

2. Next, I would tell you that Hell is *the abode of sin*. It will not be merely *past* sin that will grieve us, but there will be *actual* sin raging within us. Evil will no longer be checked and curbed as it is now; but it will have its full sway. It will be no longer in the bud; but full-blown. Oftentimes, even now, sin makes a wicked man unhappy; but then it will make his very heart ache, without the smallest hope of getting rid of it. There will be a dreadful feeling of guilt; but no place of repentance, no hope of pardon, no blood to cleanse.

3. Hell is the abode of *sorrow* too. Heaven, as we have seen, will be a sorrowless state; but Hell will be a state of unutterable woe, " where there is weeping, and wailing, and gnashing of teeth." There is grief on earth; but it is not *hopeless* grief—it is not grief *without a remedy*. Here sometimes we meet with exceeding great sorrow; but not to be compared with that sorrow which makes men (as St. John says) " gnaw their tongues for pain, and blaspheme the God of Heaven." Oh, there is not one ray of light in that dismal dungeon; but all is gloom and darkness, " the blackness of darkness for ever ! "

Of all sorrows, the sorrow of *remorse* is the bitterest—the sorrow of a guilty conscience which despairs of pardon. Have we not heard of its forcing some men to put an end to their lives? And we have been told of men too, who have been tried for some heavy offence, and acquitted, in a court of justice. And then afterwards they have given themselves up, and confessed their crime, and actually begged for death—unable to bear the gnawings of a guilty conscience. To endure such a death as King Herod died would be bad enough; for he was eaten by worms. For a man to have his flesh eaten off his bones till he died, would be dreadful indeed. But what is this to the agonies of Hell? We read of "a worm" being there "which never dies." And I take this to mean the gnawing, stinging worm of conscience.

And then there is another cause of bitterness to the lost—they will be for ever *shut out from God*. Just think what their misery will be, when those words rend their ears, "Depart from me, ye cursed"—"I never knew you; depart from me, ye workers of iniquity." Never more to see Him whose name is Love! Never more to hear the Saviour's voice! Once they *would not* come, and now they *cannot* come.

4. But not only is there sorrow in Hell, but actual *bodily suffering*. We read of the Rich man in the parable " lifting up his eyes, being *in torments*." We read of him asking for a drop of water to cool his burning tongue. We read of a " Fire which shall never be quenched ; " and of " the smoke of their torment going up for ever and ever."

Who would not tremble to see a man led away to a place of execution, and there burnt to death? Whose heart would not shudder at such a sight? But this would be as nothing compared with the torments of Hell. I would just ask you the question which Isaiah asked— ". Who among us shall dwell with the devouring fire? Who among us shall dwell with everlasting burnings?"

5. But I have one more awful truth to state concerning Hell. It is this—the sorrows and pains, and misery, of Hell will not only be greater than we can possibly imagine, but they will be *everlasting*. The Death there will be "*eternal* death." The Fire there will be "*eternal* fire"—it "*never*" shall be quenched." The Punishment there will be "*everlasting* punishment."

This it is that makes the misery of the lost *complete*. This it is that puts the topstone on their woe—IT SHALL NEVER END! Few are so tossed in this world, but they have *some* rest. There are few tempests, without *some* lull between the storms. But there is no pause in that storm which falls upon the inhabitants of Hell—"they rest not day nor night."

Oh, my Friends, think of those

words, FOR EVER! Torments *for ever!* sufferings *for ever!* lost *for ever!* We can hardly take in the idea. It is too much for us. Our minds are too narrow to grasp it. It would be hard to measure the waters of the sea: but harder still to reckon the days, and years, and ages, of a boundless eternity. Eternity is like an ocean without a shore to it— like a deep where we can find no bottom. It is a beginning without a middle or an end. After millions of years passed in it, still it will be only begun. God's wrath in Hell will be always " wrath *to come.*"

Suppose Adam had lived till now, and lived in misery and torment. Would you not say that he had endured a fearful amount of woe? Yet this is not eternity. It would be less—far less—than *everlasting* punishment.

I have now told you many things about Heaven and Hell. I know that I have described them but very poorly. But I think that if you have understood the little that I have said, surely you will become new men—it will make you very thoughtful.

Oh what a difference between the two! Heaven, the dwelling-place of God, of Jesus, of the Angels, of the saved! and Hell, the prison-house of Devils, and of the lost! Heaven, the place where sin never enters and sorrow is unknown! and Hell, the abode of wickedness and woe! The joys of the one, and the misery of the other, endless, everlasting!

And now the question comes, "*How can I escape Hell, and win Heaven? Towards which place am I at this moment hastening?*"

I have already told you in these sermons, that we are all of us by nature ruined and lost; but that Jesus has come from heaven to save the lost. Well then, the way is open to us. There is salvation for each one of us who seeks it. Christ is able and willing to deliver us from the Hell we deserve.

Yes, we have seen what a vast difference there is between Heaven and Hell. And let me tell you, there is a vast difference too between those who are bent on reaching Heaven, and those who are hurrying towards Hell.

I will try and describe to you who those are that are travelling along the broad road "that leadeth to destruction." Who are they?

All wicked ones who are living in sin, you will say. Yes, there is no doubt about them. They are journeying towards Hell. It may be said of them, as it was of wicked Judas, that they are going "to their own place." For instance, the cold-hearted Infidel, who hates the God who made him, and the Saviour who bought him with His blood—the man who speaks slightingly of God's precious Word, the Bible; and who scoffs at religion—a few years at most, and he will have his portion: the man too who is breaking God's laws, who never comes to God's house, who swears, and drinks, and follows the full bent of his own wicked ways.

But this is not all. Every *careless* one—every one who makes this world his home—who thinks more of his body than he does of his soul—who seldom prays, seldom reads his Bible—who makes game of religious people—he also is going quickly towards Hell.

We must go a step further. Every one who is only *outwardly* religious, and whose heart is not entirely given to God —the man who comes to church perhaps, and even sometimes to the Lord's Table, but has never come as a sinner to Christ—what shall we say of him? Alas! Brethren, I am afraid we must say, that he is on the broad road too.

And, again, those who have *felt a little*, and oftentimes have *resolved to go right*—who sigh, and wish they were better, and who mean, as they think, to be better some day—who plainly see that to be religious is the only way to be happy, and who envy those who are so. But there they stop—they get no further. Now, what must we say of these? They cannot be on their way to Heaven; for Christ says, "He that is not *with me* is against me." Is there no middle path then that we can say they are walking in? I know of none. Ah, they too, if they change not, must be numbered with those against whom the door of Heaven will be closed.

Who then can be saved? *Who* shall

enter that joyful, happy, holy Heaven we have been speaking of? Those who have turned away from sin and the world, and found Christ to be their Saviour—who have given their whole hearts to God. They too are sinners; but they have gone to Jesus, and obtained His pardon. They know that He died for them on the cross; and they look to Him, and feel peace. His blood has cleansed them from all their sins. They now live unto God. The Holy Spirit has changed their hearts. And they feel a delight and comfort in serving God, and walking in His ways.

Beloved Brethren, if *you* would be saved from Hell, and get to Heaven, there is but one way, but one road to walk in. Believe in Christ. Take Him for your Master. Turn your back upon every bad way. Have nothing more to do with it. Ask the Holy Spirit to make you hate sin. Ask Him to give you grace to lead a holy life; for without holiness Heaven cannot be your Home.

And now, my Friends, I have done. I have preached to you five very plain, homely sermons. I have spoken the truth to you—the bare simple truth. And I pray that God may bless it to your souls. If I have only taught you to *know* more than perhaps you did before, then I am afraid these sermons will have done you but little good. But if any one heart has *felt* more—if any one of you have felt the sting of sin in your conscience, and have gone and sought relief in Christ—if any one has resolved in real earnest to lead a new life—then I thank God with all my heart.

You and I, dear Brethren, shall soon close our eyes on this world. It is every moment slipping from under us. Oh let us not make it our resting-place. Let us hasten to secure a better rest above. And God grant that we may safely reach that blessed Home, which He has prepared for them that love Him!

LONDON: WERTHEIM, MACINTOSH, and HUNT,
24, Paternoster-row, and 23, Holles-street, Cavendish-square.

CPSIA information can be obtained
at www.ICGtesting.com
Printed in the USA
LVHW081705101121
702977LV00014B/749